CLARA BARTON

Clara Barton is born as the youngest child. She is shy – until her brother's illness teaches her about the medicine of the day. She puts this **nursing knowledge** to work when America splits in a violent **Civil War**. Barton decides that the armies without any official nurses need her **on the battlefield . . .**

WAS CLARA BARTON A SHY CHILD?

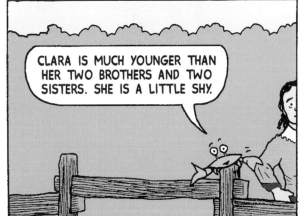

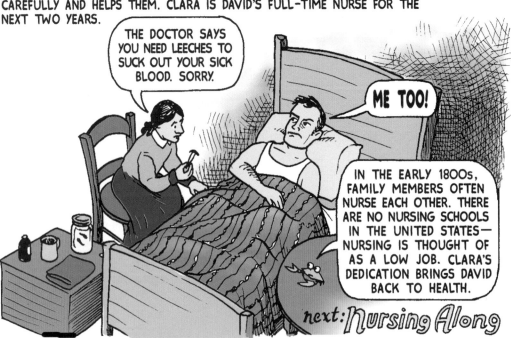

HOW DID BARTON JOIN THE CIVIL WAR?

CLARA BARTON OVERCOMES HER SHYNESS AND BECOMES A TEACHER. FROM 1836 TO 1853 SHE MAKES ROWDY CLASSROOMS INTO PEACEFUL PLACES TO LEARN.

NICE THROW, ERNIE. NOW, HOW DO YOU SPELL "POTATO?"

IN 1854, SHE MOVES TO WASHINGTON, D.C., TO WORK AS A GOVERNMENT CLERK. SHE WATCHES POLITICIANS DEBATE SLAVERY AND GET ANGRIER. IN **1861**...

oh no.

CLARA! THE SOUTHERNERS CAPTURED FORT SUMTER!

IF THERE IS NO SOLDIER'S ARM TO RAISE THE STARS AND STRIPES ABOVE OUR CAPITAL, GOD GIVE STRENGTH TO **MY** ARM!

PRESIDENT ABRAHAM LINCOLN CALLS FOR 75,000 VOLUNTEERS TO JOIN THE UNITED STATES ARMY. U.S. SOLDIERS ARE ATTACKED BY PRO-SOUTHERN PEOPLE IN BALTIMORE, MARYLAND, ON APRIL 19, 1861.

SOME OF THESE WOUNDED SOLDIERS ARE TAKEN TO THE CAPITOL BUILDING IN D.C. BARTON RUSHES TO HELP.

PLEASE, MA'AM ...ALL MY BAGS WERE LOST IN THE MOB.

I'LL FIND YOU A TOOTHBRUSH.

SHE COLLECTS DONATIONS OF CLEAN CLOTHING, HOMEMADE JAMS, AND SOAP.

SHE HAS THREE WAREHOUSES FULL OF SUPPLIES WHEN THE FIRST MAJOR BATTLE OF THE CIVIL WAR HAPPENS: THE FIRST BATTLE OF MANASSAS (BULL RUN) FLOODS D.C. WITH WOUNDED MEN.

IT... WAS AWFUL. I LAY ON THE GROUND FOR TWO DAYS WAITING FOR A DOCTOR.

I NEED TO GO WHERE I CAN DO THE MOST **GOOD!**

I MUST GET TO THE **BATTLEFIELD** NEXT!!

DID THE ARMY BAN BARTON FROM HOSPITALS?

CLARA BARTON BECOMES FAMOUS FOR DARING TO HELP SOLDIERS ON THE CIVIL WAR BATTLEFIELDS. SHE IS NOT THE **ONLY** ONE DOING THIS.

ELIZABETH BLACKWELL IS THE FIRST FEMALE DOCTOR IN AMERICA. SHE TRAINS WOMEN TO BE NURSES.

WAIT! THE SURGERY AREA MUST BE CLEANED FOR HIM FIRST!

DOROTHEA DIX IS NAMED THE UNITED STATES GOVERNMENT'S SUPERINTENDENT OF WOMEN NURSES.

I WANT ONLY WOMEN OVER 30 YEARS OLD. THEY MUST BE SERIOUS OF MIND AND PLAIN-LOOKING.

BARTON DOES NOT LIKE TO WORK UNDER SOMEONE ELSE'S CONTROL.

I CAN DO MORE IF I AM FREE TO GO WHERE I SEE THE GREATEST NEED.

HOLD IT!

WE ARE BETTER ORGANIZED NOW THAN AT THE WAR'S BEGINNING. WE DON'T **NEED** YOU.

WRONG! YOU STILL EXPECT SOLDIERS TO WORK **16** HOURS A DAY WITH ONLY WORMY CRACKERS, STALE BEEF, AND WARM WATER!!

WE HAVE HEARD ENOUGH OF YOUR CRITICISM, MISS BARTON. YOU ARE BANNED FROM ARMY HOSPITALS!

BARTON WALKS THE STREETS OF FREDERICKSBURG, VIRGINIA, AFTER A NEARBY BATTLE.

WHY ARE WOUNDED MEN STILL OUT HERE??

OUR OFFICERS WON'T LET US PUT THEM IN THE NICE HOUSES IN THIS TOWN.

BARTON QUICKLY TAKES A TRAIN TO WASHINGTON, D.C., TO TELL THIS TO A FRIEND IN THE U.S. SENATE.

BAH! WE HAVE NO REPORTS OF SUCH "SUFFERING."

I BELIEVE BARTON. GET SOLDIERS SHELTER OR I'LL HAVE THE SENATE INVESTIGATE!

next: **RED BADGE** *of* **COURAGE**

WHO BEGINS THE AMERICAN RED CROSS?

AFTER THE AMERICAN CIVIL WAR, **CLARA BARTON** GOES TO EUROPE. IN 1870, WHEN FRANCE DECLARES WAR ON PRUSSIA, BARTON HELPS A NEW GROUP CALLED THE RED CROSS.

AMAZING! YOU ARE WELL-ORGANIZED AND TRAINED! HOW DID...

PEOPLE FROM MANY COUNTRIES PREPARE IN PEACETIME TO HELP DURING WAR. WHY HASN'T THE UNITED STATES JOINED?

BARTON RETURNS TO AMERICA TO ASK POLITICIANS THAT QUESTION.

WE WILL NOT SIGN ANY TREATY THAT MIGHT MAKE US FIGHT A WAR IN EUROPE. WE ARE **TIRED** OF WAR!

THEY DON'T UNDERSTAND. THE RED CROSS WILL **REDUCE** SUFFERING, NOT CAUSE IT! I MUST **PROVE** THAT!

IN **1881** SHE BEGINS THE **FIRST** CHAPTER OF THE AMERICAN ASSOCIATION OF THE RED CROSS.

BARTON ALSO EXPANDS THE RED CROSS MISSION BEYOND WAR. SHE WANTS TO HELP PEOPLE HURT BY **NATURAL DISASTERS**: HURRICANES, EARTHQUAKES, FIRES...

...AND **FLOODS!!** SHE AND RED CROSS WORKERS SPEND FIVE MONTHS HELPING VICTIMS OF THE **1889** FLOOD IN JOHNSTOWN, PENNSYLVANIA.

WHEN BARTON GOES TO THE THIRD INTERNATIONAL CONFERENCE OF THE RED CROSS, SHE IS THE **FIRST WOMAN** TO BE A DIPLOMATIC REPRESENTATIVE OF THE U.S. HER WORK ALSO CONVINCES THE U.S. TO SIGN THE TREATY SUPPORTING THE RED CROSS. **END**

CHAPTER 2

HARRIET TUBMAN

Harriet Tubman is born a **slave** on a **Maryland** plantation. She is injured by a heavy weight and will have dizziness and blackouts the rest of her life. But that does not stop her from running north to freedom on the "**Underground Railroad**." And it does not stop her from going back to the South to **rescue other slaves**. How many can she save before she is recaptured?

WHERE DID HARRIET TUBMAN GROW UP?

ON MARYLAND'S EASTERN SHORE IN **1831**...

Gotcha!

ARE YOU SURE??

AAH! A TALKING CRAB!?!

WHY ARE YOU TRYING TO TAKE MY FREEDOM? **YOU** KNOW IT IS NOT FAIR!

UMM, I WAS JUST PLAYING AROUND. I WASN'T GOING TO MAKE YOU A PET OR ANYTHING.

THAT'S OK, HARRIET. BUT REMEMBER: FREEDOM IS NOT A GAME.

CHESTER FOLLOWS THE 11-YEAR-OLD SLAVE BACK TO THE BRODAS PLANTATION NEAR BUCKTOWN, **MARYLAND**.

HARRIET! YOU HEAR? SLAVE NAMED **NAT TURNER** KILLED HIS MASTER IN VIRGINIA. HE IS REBELLING FOR FREEDOM!

NO ONE KNOWS IF TURNER WILL STAY IN VIRGINIA OR TAKE THE UNDERGROUND RAILROAD NORTH.

FIRST A TALKING CRAB. NOW A RAILROAD THAT GOES UNDERGROUND? WHAT IS GOING ON??!

TURNER IS CAPTURED AND KILLED. BUT OTHER SOUTHERN SLAVES STILL TRY TO RUN AWAY.

STOP HIM!

YOU LET HIM GET AWAY, GIRL!

KRAK

HARRIET!

next: RUNAWAY

DID SPELLS STOP HARRIET TUBMAN?

ON MARYLAND'S EASTERN SHORE IN 1849...

...OH, MY HEAD... WH-WHAT HAPPENED?

YOU HAD ANOTHER BLACKOUT, **HARRIET TUBMAN**. EVER SINCE YOU GOT HIT ON THE HEAD WITH THAT IRON WEIGHT YEARS AGO, YOUR SPELLS HAVE GOTTEN **WORSE**.

WELL, THOSE SPELLS WON'T STOP **ME**. I HAVE TO GET FREE!

YOU COULD FAINT WHEN YOU RUN FROM THE BOUNTY HUNTERS!

I WILL SURVIVE. MY DADDY TAUGHT ME ABOUT LIVING IN THE WOODS ON JUST BERRIES AND RABBITS. HE SHOWED ME HOW TO GO NORTH BY FOLLOWING THE **NORTH STAR**.

MY HUSBAND, JOHN TUBMAN, DOES NOT WANT TO GO. BUT **I MUST BE FREE** *OR DIE!*

HARRIET WADES THROUGH THE CHOPTANK RIVER. THIS HIDES HER SCENT FROM HUNTING DOGS THAT TRACK ESCAPED SLAVES. SHE HIDES AT DAY AND WALKS AT NIGHT.

SUDDENLY...

DOOWHHHmm

HOURS LATER, SHE WAKENS AND HEARS:

WHERE COULD THAT SLAVE BE??

LET'S GO. NO RUNAWAY ON THIS ROAD.

Shhh

TUBMAN REACHES CAMDEN, **DELAWARE**, JUST AS THE SUN IS RISING...

COME IN, DEAR. YOU ARE SAFE IN OUR QUAKER HOME. YOU ARE ON THE **UNDERGROUND RAILROAD** NOW!

THREE DAYS LATER, THE QUAKERS TAKE HER TO WOODS NORTH OF TOWN AND SEND HER TO THE NEXT "CONDUCTOR."

LOOK FOR A MAN IN A GRAVEYARD!

next: **THE FUGITIVE**

WHAT WAS HARRIET TUBMAN'S REWARD?

Harriet Tubman

SHOWS **COURAGE**. AFTER HER ESCAPE FROM SLAVERY, IT WOULD BE EASY FOR HER TO LIVE THE REST OF HER LIFE **FREE** IN CANADA.

BUT SHE RISKS HER **OWN** FREEDOM TO GO BACK TO MARYLAND TO FREE **OTHER** SLAVES!

I HAVE HEARD MY PEOPLE'S GROANS. I HAVE SEEN THEIR TEARS. I WOULD GIVE **EVERY** **DROP** OF MY BLOOD TO FREE THEM!

SHE OFTEN HIDES IN PLAIN SIGHT OF SLAVE HUNTERS.

$40,000 HARRIET TUBMAN

SHE KNOWS NO WHITE PERSON WILL SUSPECT A BLACK WOMAN WALKING SOUTH, BACK **INTO** THE SLAVE STATES.

ONE DAY SHE EVEN CROSSES PATHS WITH HER OLD OWNER, DOC THOMPSON. SHE ACTS FOOLISH TO TRICK HIM.

OOH! EEK! My Chickens! Help!

Hee HAW HAW!

BOYD '02

IN **1857**, SHE RETURNS TO MARYLAND TO FREE HER PARENTS.

Go down, Moses, Way down in Egypt land...

IT'S HARRIET AGAIN! SHE'S COME TO LEAD US OUT OF CAPTIVITY, JUST LIKE **MOSES** DID IN THE BIBLE!

HER FATHER IS IN JAIL FOR HELPING OTHER SLAVES ESCAPE. TUBMAN GETS SOMEONE TO SAW HER DAD OUT.

HER PARENTS ARE IN THEIR 70s, TOO OLD TO GO THROUGH SWAMPS TO FREEDOM. TUBMAN MAKES A CART.

CATCHERS WILL LOOK FOR THREE SLAVES, NOT TWO. I WILL WALK IN THE WOODS AND MEET YOU LATER.

THANKS, "MOSES!"

next: **harriet** the **SPY**

WHAT DID TUBMAN DO IN THE WAR?

ON 1858, **HARRIET TUBMAN** MEETS **JOHN BROWN**.

I PLAN TO RAID SOUTHERN PLANTATIONS TO FREE SLAVES. **YOU** CAN GUIDE THOSE SLAVES NORTH TO FREEDOM FOR ME!

YOU CAN COUNT ON ME!

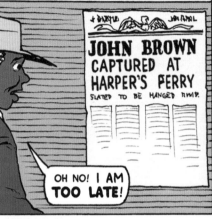

TUBMAN GETS SICK FOR SEVERAL MONTHS. WHEN SHE IS WELL, SHE STARTS SOUTH TO HELP BROWN...

JOHN BROWN CAPTURED AT HARPER'S FERRY

SLATED TO BE HANGED TIME.

OH NO! I AM **TOO LATE!**

TUBMAN MAKES HER LAST TRIP ON "**THE UNDERGROUND RAILROAD**" IN 1861. IN 19 TRIPS, SHE HAS LED MORE THAN **300** SLAVES TO FREEDOM.

I NEVER LOST **ONE** TO THE SLAVE CATCHERS!

THE **CIVIL WAR** BEGINS. TUBMAN GOES TO SOUTH CAROLINA TO SPY FOR THE NORTHERN ARMY IN 1862.

I AM THE ONE CALLED "**MOSES**." TRUST ME. WHERE ARE THE CONFEDERATE SOLDIERS??

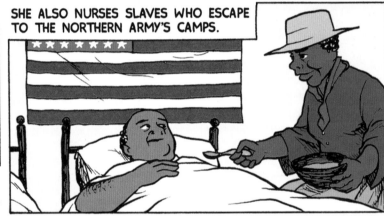

SHE ALSO NURSES SLAVES WHO ESCAPE TO THE NORTHERN ARMY'S CAMPS.

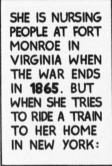

SHE IS NURSING PEOPLE AT FORT MONROE IN VIRGINIA WHEN THE WAR ENDS IN **1865.** BUT WHEN SHE TRIES TO RIDE A TRAIN TO HER HOME IN NEW YORK:

YOU CANNOT SIT **HERE!**

I HAVE A PASS FROM THE ARMY! I HAVE BEEN IN THE WAR!

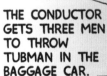

THE CONDUCTOR GETS THREE MEN TO THROW TUBMAN IN THE BAGGAGE CAR.

HMMPH! THIS ISN'T MUCH BETTER THAN BEING ON THE "UNDERGROUND RAILROAD" **BEFORE** THE WAR!!

TUBMAN FIGHTS FOR JUSTICE UNTIL HER DEATH IN 1913! END

SUSAN B. ANTHONY

Susan B. Anthony is bothered that so many people fight to free African-Americans from slavery but will not fight to free **women** from their legal bonds. She begins a campaign to win women the **right to vote** and to own their own property. And she may go to jail for trying to vote in the **presidential election of 1872** . . .

WHO WAS SUSAN B. ANTHONY?

CHESTER, I LOST A TOOTH! AND THE TOOTH FAIRY LEFT ME THIS. WHAT IS IT?!

LISA, THAT IS A SUSAN B. ANTHONY DOLLAR. IT MUST BE TIME TO PLAY SHOW ME WHO IS ON THE MONEY

BROYD '00

BEFORE THE CIVIL WAR, AMERICAN WOMEN CANNOT VOTE OR RUN FOR POLITICAL OFFICE. THE CULTURE OF THE TIME SAYS WOMEN SHOULD RAISE CHILDREN AND CLEAN THEIR HOUSE, NOT RUN A BUSINESS OR HOLD A PAYING JOB.

BUT **QUAKERS** BELIEVE MEN AND WOMEN ARE EQUAL. ANTHONY IS BORN IN **1820** TO QUAKERS. SHE HAS AN AUNT WHO PREACHES — THOUGH AT THIS TIME OTHER AMERICAN WOMEN CANNOT SPEAK PUBLICLY.

ANTHONY GROWS UP TO BE A TEACHER — ONE OF THE FEW JOBS OPEN TO WOMEN.

HERE IS YOUR PAY: $2.50 FOR THE WEEK.

BUT— BUT THE MAN WHO HAD THIS JOB BEFORE ME GOT $10!!

SHE ALSO LEARNS THAT MARRIED WOMEN HAVE LITTLE CONTROL OVER THE MONEY **THEY** EARN. IN **1855** SHE STARTS A PETITION ASKING NEW YORK'S STATE LEGISLATURE TO GIVE WOMEN LEGAL CONTROL OF THEIR PROPERTY AND CHILDREN.

HHMPPF! YOU SHOULD BE HOME HAVING KIDS!

IT IS BETTER FOR ME TO HELP WOMEN GET CONTROL OF THE CHILDREN THEY ALREADY HAVE!

SHE FAILS TO CONVINCE THE MALE POLITICIANS IN **1854** AND **1855** AND **1856** AND **1857** AND **1858** AND **1859**

IN **1860** THE NEW YORK STATE LEGISLATURE FINALLY PASSES "THE MARRIED WOMEN'S PROPERTY ACT."

OUR FIRST BIG WIN, ELIZABETH CADY STANTON!! BUT OTHER PEOPLE NEED OUR HELP NOW...

next: TUBMAN AND DOUGLASS

WHAT WAS THE UNDERGROUND RAILROAD?

HURRY, GIRL! WE HAVE TO GET TO **SUSAN ANTHONY'S** HOUSE — THEY MAY BE FOLLOWING US!

BOYD '00

MISS ANTHONY! THANK THE STARS YOU'RE HOME! WE HAD A ROUGH RUN TONIGHT.

WELL, **HARRIET TUBMAN**, IT WAS YOU WHO TOLD ME THE **UNDERGROUND RAILROAD** IS NO FREE RIDE.

YOU CAN REST IN MY ATTIC. TOMORROW WE WILL SNEAK YOU FROM ROCHESTER, N.Y., INTO CANADA!

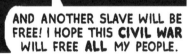

AND ANOTHER SLAVE WILL BE FREE! I HOPE THIS **CIVIL WAR** WILL FREE **ALL** MY PEOPLE.

HI!

LISA, YOU ARE MEETING TWO OF THE MOST FAMOUS WOMEN IN 1800s AMERICA. TUBMAN IS THE "MOSES OF HER PEOPLE" FOR HELPING HUNDREDS OF SLAVES.

AND SUSAN BROWNELL ANTHONY IS TRYING TO FREE ANOTHER KIND OF SLAVE...

FREDERICK DOUGLASS, YOU AND I BOTH NEED THE RIGHT TO VOTE — "SUFFRAGE!" WITHOUT A VOTE, WE WILL NEVER HAVE FREEDOM.

RIGHT ON, SUSAN B.!

ALL THAT MAKES MAN INTELLIGENT IS **EQUALLY** TRUE OF WOMAN!

EXACTLY! WE NEED TO ORGANIZE AND PUSH FOR AN AMENDMENT TO THE U.S. CONSTITUTION TO GET THE VOTE!

next: THE CRIME OF VOTING

15

DID ANTHONY GET A FAIR TRIAL?

MISS SUSAN B. ANTHONY, YOU ARE **UNDER ARREST FOR VOTING** IN ROCHESTER, N.Y.!

BALLOTS HERE

GOOD — LET'S ARGUE THIS IN COURT! YOU KNOW, THAT "B" IN MY NAME STANDS FOR **"BUZZ-SAW!"**

HUNDREDS OF PEOPLE COME TO HER TRIAL IN JUNE **1873**...

IF MISS ANTHONY'S BROTHER VOTES, SOCIETY CALLS THAT **HONORABLE**. BUT A WOMAN VOTING IS **CRIMINAL?!** THIS IS NOT FAIR!

♪♫

uhhh, SIR?

YOUR HONOR?

SORRY, I WAS GOING OVER THE VERDICT I WROTE YESTERDAY. HOW DOES THIS SOUND:

GUILTY!

YOU WON'T LET THE JURY MAKE ITS OWN DECISION?! THIS IS **TYRANNY!!**

SIT DOWN! THIS COURT ORDERS YOU TO PAY A FINE OF $100!

I SHALL NEVER PAY **ONE DOLLAR** OF YOUR UNJUST PENALTY!!

MEANWHILE... ANOTHER WOMAN WHO TRIED TO VOTE TAKES HER CASE TO THE **U.S. SUPREME COURT.** THE COURT SAYS STATES CAN MAKE THEIR OWN VOTING RULES.

THIS PRACTICE HURTS WOMEN **AND** BLACKS BECAUSE SOUTHERN STATES USE POLL TAXES AND LITERACY TESTS TO KEEP PEOPLE FROM VOTING.

next: **WYOMING**

17

WHEN DID ALL WOMEN GET TO VOTE?

CHAPTER 4

HELEN KELLER

Helen Keller is a lively Alabama baby, but at age two an illness takes her **eyesight** and her **hearing**. Keller is trapped in a lonely, silent world with few ways to communicate. In 1887, **Anne Sullivan** finally reaches the six-year-old. Sullivan's lessons will open Keller to the world – and the world to Keller . . .

HOW DID HELEN KELLER GO BLIND?

NOTHING.

YOU SEE NOTHING.

YOU HEAR NOTHING.

YOU CANNOT SPEAK A WORD.

YOU ARE A SIX-YEAR-OLD GIRL NAMED HELEN KELLER.

BOYD'01

:sigh: HELEN WAS SO BRIGHT AND LIVELY AS A BABY.

SHE GOT SICK BEFORE SHE WAS TWO YEARS OLD. HELEN HAD A HIGH FEVER AND ALMOST DIED.

THE DISEASE TOOK HER EYESIGHT AND HER HEARING. NOW HELEN'S SENSE OF TOUCH IS HER MAIN LINK TO THE WORLD.

HELEN! THAT'S MY FOOD!

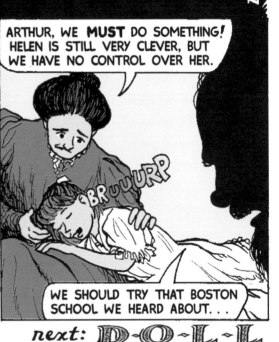

ARTHUR, WE MUST DO SOMETHING! HELEN IS STILL VERY CLEVER, BUT WE HAVE NO CONTROL OVER HER.

BRUUURP

WE SHOULD TRY THAT BOSTON SCHOOL WE HEARD ABOUT...

next: D-O-L-L

WHO WAS HELEN KELLER'S TEACHER?

IN MARCH 1887, ANNE SULLIVAN COMES TO HELEN KELLER'S HOME IN ALABAMA.

MR. KELLER, WHAT IS HELEN DOING??

IMITATING AN ICE CREAM MAKER. SHE WANTS ICE CREAM. SHE USES ABOUT 60 SYMBOLS TO COMMUNICATE.

SHE DOES NOT UNDERSTAND WHAT WORDS ARE. SHE CANNOT HEAR OR SEE. HELEN NEEDS LANGUAGE — A WAY TO SHARE IDEAS AND THOUGHTS WITH OTHERS.

BOYD '01

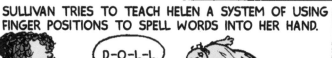

SULLIVAN TRIES TO TEACH HELEN A SYSTEM OF USING FINGER POSITIONS TO SPELL WORDS INTO HER HAND.

D-O-L-L.

KRIHK

SHE IS AS WILD AS A HORSE! SHE KNOCKED OUT MY FRONT TEETH!

MR. KELLER, I CANNOT TEACH HELEN UNLESS I CAN DISCIPLINE HER.

MAYBE STAYING AT THIS COTTAGE AWAY FROM HER FAMILY WILL HELP HER CONCENTRATE. I MUST PROVE TO HER THAT EACH **THING** HAS A **NAME**!

next: W-A-T-E-R

HOW DID HELEN KELLER WRITE?

HELEN KELLER CANNOT SEE OR HEAR. BUT BY AGE 12 SHE LEARNS TO WRITE CAREFULLY AGAINST A RULER.

If a fairy made me choose sight or touch, I would not part with the warm contact of human hands.

THE TROUBLE: SHE CANNOT PROOFREAD WHAT SHE HAS WRITTEN.

LET'S TRY **BRAILLE**. A FRENCH MAN MADE THIS SYSTEM OF RAISED DOTS TO REPRESENT LETTERS.

KELLER

CAN NOW READ HER OWN WRITING!

AT 16, THIS SOUTHERNER GOES TO A GIRLS SCHOOL IN BOSTON. SHE TAKES ROMAN HISTORY, MATH, FRENCH...

SHE INSISTS ON TAKING THE ENTRANCE TEST FOR RADCLIFFE COLLEGE, THE SISTER SCHOOL TO HARVARD.

"14: WHERE ARE ARBELA, CORYERE, DACIA, LADE, RUBICON, AND WITH WHAT EVENT IS EACH CONNECTED?"

KELLER PASSES WITH HIGH SCORES. BUT THE RADCLIFFE BOARD IS UNSURE...

COULD SHE STUDY ON HER OWN? WE HAVE NO EQUIPMENT TO MEET HER NEEDS.

I KNOW HOW TO GET ALONG. I WILL SURVIVE!

SHE GRADUATES WITH HONORS FOUR YEARS LATER!

A MAGAZINE ASKS KELLER TO WRITE HER AUTOBIOGRAPHY. IN **1903** SHE PUBLISHES "THE STORY OF MY LIFE."

THE BOOK IS A HIT. KELLER IS FAMOUS!

next: W·O·R·L·D

HOW DID KELLER HELP THE DISABLED?

HELEN KELLER IS FAMOUS ALL OVER THE WORLD FOR OVERCOMING HER DEAFNESS AND BLINDNESS.

SHE PUSHES FOR WOMEN TO GET THE RIGHT TO VOTE.

AMERICAN WOMEN GET THE VOTE IN 1920.

SHE WRITES THAT AMERICA SHOULD NOT FIGHT IN WORLD WAR I. SHE BECOMES A SOCIALIST WHO DEFENDS WORKER RIGHTS.

"I HAVE VISITED SWEATSHOPS, FACTORIES, CROWDED SLUMS. IF I COULD NOT SEE IT, I COULD SMELL IT."

KELLER ALSO URGES THE WORLD TO ADOPT JUST ONE READING SYSTEM FOR THE BLIND. WHEN SHE GREW UP, THERE WERE FIVE!

FORGET NEW YORK POINT AND MOON POINT! LET'S ALL USE BRAILLE!

KELLER TRAVELS TO MANY COUNTRIES. IN A 1937 VISIT TO JAPAN, SHE IS THE FIRST WOMAN EVER ALLOWED TO TOUCH ONE CITY'S SACRED BUDDHA STATUE.

SHE MEETS MANY PRESIDENTS AND WORLD LEADERS — SOME OF THEM BLIND LIKE HER!

GOD GAVE US LOUIS BRAILLE FOR ONE EYE AND HELEN KELLER FOR THE OTHER!

SHE CONVINCES HANDICAPPED PRESIDENT FRANKLIN D. ROOSEVELT TO LET BLIND PEOPLE RUN NEWSPAPER STANDS IN GOVERNMENT BUILDINGS.

ANYTHING HELEN KELLER IS FOR, **I** AM FOR!

AFTER INSPIRING MILLIONS OVER MANY DECADES, KELLER DIES JUNE 1, 1968.

BOYD '01

END